Wounded by God's People

Discovering How God's Love Heals Our Hearts

Anne Graham Lotz

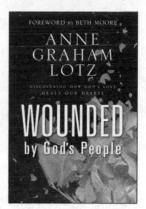

Tucked into Abraham's biography is the story of Hagar, an Egyptian slave who bore Abraham his son Ishmael. Exiled, abused, and often overlooked, Hagar suffered greatly at the hands of those who considered themselves God's people. Though some of her pain was the result of her own poor choices, there is no doubt that the emotional and spiritual wounds inflicted upon her by those who claimed to follow the one true God scarred her deeply.

Anne Graham Lotz brings the life of Hagar into astonishing relevance. As her story unfolds, you will discover how time and again God acts to help those who have been hurt. But while Anne identifies with the wounded, the unpleasant reality is that she also identifies with the wounders because she has been one too. She knows from experience that wounding is a cycle that needs to be broken. And by God's grace, it can be.

Many have had similar experiences. Maybe you are among those who have been so deeply hurt by the church that you no longer want anything to do with God. Perhaps you are a wounder living in a self-imposed exile, believing yourself unworthy to be restored to a warm, loving relationship with God or His followers. Whatever your hurts may be, *Wounded by God's People* helps you begin a healing journey—one that enables you to reclaim the joy of God's presence and all the blessings God has for you.

God loves the wounded. And the wounders.

Available in stores and online!

Fixing My Eyes on Jesus

Daily Moments in His Word

Anne Graham Lotz

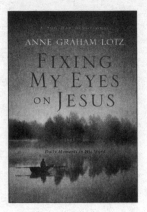

The whole Bible points to Jesus. We need to keep our eyes on Jesus, who both began and finished this race we're in (Hebrews 12:2).

In *Fixing My Eyes on Jesus*, from award-winning author Anne Graham Lotz, you will read a Scripture and inspirational devotion for each day of the year that will encourage, uplift, renew, and challenge you on your spiritual walk with Jesus.

A perfect size for carrying with you on the go, in a beautiful package that also makes this a gorgeous gift for a friend or family member, *Fixing My Eyes on Jesus* is the spiritual nourishment you crave.

Available in stores and online!

Expecting to See Jesus

A Wake-Up Call for God's People

Anne Graham Lotz

Expecting to See Jesus—the expanded edition of *I Saw the Lord*—is the result of Anne Graham Lotz's life lived in the hope of Jesus' return. As you journey with her through the pages of the Bible, you'll come to realize why she lives her life expecting to see Jesus at any minute.

And she wants to make sure you and all other Christians are ready for that moment when your faith becomes sight.

Anne knows from personal experience that it's in the busyness of our days, as we're drifting in comfortable complacency, that we most need a wake-up call—a jolt that pushes us to seek out a revival of our passion for Jesus that began as a blazing fire but somehow has died down to an ineffective glow.

In *Expecting to See Jesus*, Anne points out the biblical signs she sees in the world all around us and shows how you can experience an authentic, deeper, richer relationship with God in a life-changing, fire-blazing revival.

Also Available:

Expecting to See Jesus Curriculum

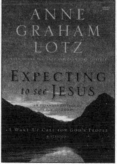

Available in stores and online!

ZONDERVAN®

The Magnificent Obsession

Embracing the God-Filled Life

Anne Graham Lotz

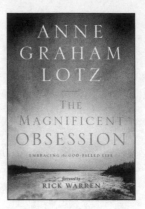

If you or someone close to you is devoted to their church but still struggles to find meaning and passion in their faith; who loves their family, works hard, contributes to their community, but still feels life is somehow incomplete and hollow at the core; who is restless in spirit, with a nagging sense that there must be something more ... there is *The Magnificent Obsession*.

Gifted Bible teacher Anne Graham Lotz, daughter of evangelist Billy Graham, has known these struggles herself. As she studied Scripture, looking for a way out of the emptiness, she found her answer in the amazing story of Abraham, a very ordinary man who became extraordinary for one pivotal reason: he pursued God in a life of obedient faith, not knowing where that decision would take him.

Anne followed Abraham's lead and began a lifelong pursuit of knowing God as He truly is, in an intensely personal relationship. Through personal anecdotes, unforgettable stories, and God-inspired insights, she invites you to draw closer to God, who is as committed to you as He was to Abraham, and longs to call you "friend."

Also by Anne Graham Lotz

ANNE
GRAHAM
LOTZ

ANGEL MINISTRIES

Anne Graham Lotz calls people to establish a personal relationship with God through Jesus Christ, then helps them develop and maintain a vibrant faith through His Word.

By visiting www.annegrahamlotz.com, you'll find free devotionals, video resources, and more from Anne's extensive library. Also available are studies in God's Word and access to free Bible study curricula for group and individual studies.

EXPECTING *to see* JESUS

A WAKE-UP CALL FOR GOD'S PEOPLE

ANNE GRAHAM LOTZ

with Henry Blackaby and Crawford Loritts

ZONDERVAN®

ZONDERVAN.com/
AUTHORTRACKER
follow your favorite authors

We want to hear from you. Please send your comments about this book to us in care of zreview@zondervan.com. Thank you.

Expecting to See Jesus Participant's Guide
Copyright © 2007, 2011 by Anne Graham Lotz

Requests for information should be addressed to:

Zondervan, *Grand Rapids, Michigan 49530*

ISBN 978-0-310-68299-8

Published in association with the literary agency of Alive Communications, Inc., 7680 Goddard Street, Suite 200, Colorado Springs, CO 80920.

Material compiled by John Tolsma, Knowledge Launch, 2607 Kingston Pike, Suite 1, Knoxville, TN 37919.

Cover photography: Ron Stroud/Masterfile®
Interior design: Sherri L. Hoffman

Printed in the United States of America

HB 01.07.2021

Contents

About Anne Graham Lotz

Anne Graham Lotz, founder of AnGeL Ministries, has passionately proclaimed God's Word to people around the world for over thirty years. Her gripping narratives and heart-touching teaching have inspired listeners in arenas and prison cells, stadiums and Bible studies, sanctuaries and seminaries, the United Nations and Amsterdam 2000. The daughter of Dr. and Mrs. Billy Graham, Anne launched *Just Give Me Jesus* in the year 2000. Anne is an award-winning and bestselling author. Her eleven books include her signature books *Just Give Me Jesus* and *The Magnificent Obsession*. Anne and her husband, Dr. Dan Lotz, reside in North Carolina. Information on Anne's ministry can be found at www.annegrahamlotz.com.

Preface

Have you ever missed a wake-up call? Several years ago, it happened to me while delivering a session at the Billy Graham Training Center at The Cove, where we filmed this series.

I had been speaking in back-to-back sessions for three days, and the night before the final day I collapsed into bed, dead to the world before my head hit the pillow . . .

Eventually, the brilliant rays of the not-so-early morning sunlight coming through the blinds pried my sleeping eyes open. As I lay in bed, enjoying the warmth of the down comforter, my mind began to stir before my body did. My first thought was, *Why is the sun up so early?* Then my body stirred, and I rolled over to look at the clock. It said 7:30! For a moment I lay in stunned stupor — then I hit the floor with a muffled, "Oh, no!"

You can imagine the rest. I missed my first speaking session and spent the remainder of my day catching up from being so out of sync.

Have you ever slept through your alarm? Have you slept on, oblivious to what time it was and missed something you were supposed to do? Or someone you were supposed to see? Or a place you were supposed to go?

I have learned the hard way that I need literal wake-up calls so I don't miss something important. But, from time to time, I also need personal wake-up calls in my own life.

Sometimes, in the busyness of my days, or the duties of my ministry, or the familiar habits of my worship, or the everyday routine of my home, I doze off in my relationship with God. That's when I most need a wake-up call—a jolt that pushes me to seek out a revival of the passion that began as a blazing, powerful fire but somehow tends to die down to a comfortable but weak, ineffective glow.

Therefore, it's my joy to invite you to participate in this video-based Bible study series. I pray it will wake you up to an authentic, deep, rich, more vibrant relationship with God.

I have been joined in this series by two dear friends, Henry Blackaby and Crawford Loritts. We invite you as, together, we consider some of the Bible's greatest examples of those who experienced personal revival in their relationships with God. For each session you'll have a Bible passage you'll study on your own. Then, to complement your personal study, you'll sit in on our DVD dialogue as we discuss the passage and what it means to live it out.

To get the most out of your personal assignments, in the second session you'll join me in a Bible study workshop where I'll teach you a simple method I use each day in my own devotions — so that you can more effectively read God's Word, listening for Him to speak to you personally through its pages.

This study is designed to be a road map for your journey toward a vibrant faith, a revived heart, and a fresh encounter with God. My prayer is that as you read His Word for yourself, share in our videotaped discussions, and discuss the lesson in your small group, you will be able to exclaim

"I'm expecting and ready to see Jesus—
I'm not sleeping
I'm awake—
My eyes are open
My heart is broken
My knees are bent
I say, Yes, Lord, yes
Mold me, move me, use me ... for Your glory."

ANNE GRAHAM LOTZ

About the Study

This participant's guide is designed to be used with the video course *Expecting to See Jesus: A Wake-Up Call for God's People*. An integral part of this course is a format for Bible study that serves as the basis for both small group use (Bible study classes, women's or men's groups, home or neighborhood studies, one-on-one discipleship) and individual use. Believing that God speaks to us through His Word, this guide teaches you how to listen as it leads you through a series of questions. The questions enable you not only to discover for yourself the eternal truths revealed by God in the Bible, but also to hear God speaking personally through His Word. You are then prepared to view a video presentation by Anne and her guests, followed by your own participation in a meaningful small group experience as you discuss the same Scripture.

Individual Study

Each session of *Expecting to See Jesus: A Wake-Up Call for God's People* features personal study. Session 1 is unique, because the personal study will occur *after* viewing the video and *after* the small group discussion. Session 2 is a Bible study workshop.

In sessions 3–9, the format will be the same: for each session, you will be assigned Scripture passages for personal study. Then, having done the personal study on your own, you will meet with your small group for a video presentation, followed by discussion on the same passages of Scripture.

Effective daily Bible study will occur if you:

- Set aside a regular place *and* a regular time for personal Bible study.
- Pray before beginning the day's assignment, asking God to speak to you through His Word.
- Write out your answers for each step in sequence.
- Make the time to be still and listen, reflecting thoughtfully on your response in the final step.

7

- Don't rush. It may take you several days of prayerful meditation on a given passage to discover meaningful lessons and hear God speaking to you. The object is not to get through the material, but to develop a meaningful relationship with God as you learn to listen to His voice.

Spiritual discipline is an essential part of a person's ability to grow in his or her relationship with God through knowledge and understanding of His Word. Take your personal study seriously and allow God to speak to you from His Word.

Group Study

Expecting to See Jesus: A Wake-Up Call for God's People includes the Matthew 24 opening video message by Anne Graham Lotz, the Bible study workshop, and seven additional sessions. Therefore, the study can be completed in nine weekly sessions, nine monthly sessions, or any schedule your group determines is best. Each session will take 60 minutes, including the video presentation and group discussion.

Space is provided in the participant's guide for you to take notes during each video presentation. After the presentation, your group facilitator will lead a discussion using the leader's guide included with the DVD. If the group is large (12 members or more), the facilitator may divide the large group, using moderators to facilitate each small group.

He's Coming!

Could this be the generation that will experience the second coming of the Son of God to earth? Years ago, it struck me that one day there would come a generation that was the last one. How would that generation know it? To my mind came Jesus' own words to His disciples. Again and again, He instructed His disciples to not be deceived, to keep watch, to not let His return come like a thief in the night.[1] In other words, He was clearly indicating that the last generation of human history, the generation that would precede and witness His return to earth, could know it IF they were diligent to not only be familiar with the signs He gave, but to also watch for them.

Expecting to See Jesus, pg. 22

Knowing the accurate time of day is critical for me in my busy schedule. Catching a plane, speaking in a pulpit, talking on a TV camera, turning in a manuscript — even cooking dinner — requires an awareness of time. Almost every room in my house has a clock, several of which are radio-activated, so that the time is accurate to the second. I would never travel without my radio-activated alarm that automatically synchronizes the time according to the zone I am in. Otherwise I may be *deceived* into missing an appointment or being too early or running too late — or burning the pot roast.

Just as I want to know what time of day it is, I also want to know what time it is in human history. If we are living "five-minutes-to-midnight," I don't want to be sleeping! I want to be familiar with the signs that Jesus gave, look for them as I read, watch, or listen to the local, national, and world news, and then get ready! Wake up! He is coming! *He's coming!*

Knowing that He's coming, and knowing what time it is in human history, can radically change your perspective on just about everything! Our attitude toward prosperity and pain, success and stress, blessing and betrayal, acclamation and abandonment, wealth and poverty, goals and grief, all change in the light of His return! This life and this planet are not all there is!

This perspective is dramatically reflected in an email our ministry received from a woman who has been praying to bring our revival ministry, *Just Give Me Jesus,* to

---

1. Matthew 24:4, 42–44.

her city. Shortly after organizing a prayer team to undergird her exploratory efforts, she was diagnosed with cancer. These were her words:

> It is really exciting and special to be getting small glimpses of how God is weaving my cancer treatment "for good" into His plans for revival. The new cancer clinic where I am getting my chemo sits near the arena. I can see it from my chemo room that has big beautiful windows producing a wonderful setting for praying for revival. Also, much of the support staff gives me much opportunity to pray and witness, invite and involve ... not sure what God will do, but sensed today He might be up to something BIG to His glory! Rejoicing in the faithful provisions of our great God![2]

This beloved woman knows what time it is! She's not wasting a moment in whining, worrying, wondering, or asking God, "Why me?" She has His kingdom agenda uppermost on her mind and is fully committed to living out her life for His glory!

The thrilling, living hope that Christians have is that the end of the world as we know it will climax with Jesus Christ coming again to this earth! There is indeed a generation that will be the last one. One in every twenty verses in the New Testament refers to this truth! Jesus Himself promised the disciples, *I will come back.*[3] When He ascended into heaven, the disciples were gazing up into the clouds where He had disappeared *when suddenly two men dressed in white stood beside them. "Men of Galilee," they said, "why do you stand here looking into the sky? This same Jesus, who has been taken from you into heaven, will come back in the same way you have seen him go into heaven."*[4]

Jesus is coming! Which means that one day ...

wrong will be set right,

love will triumph over hate,

good will win out over evil,

wars will cease,

guns will silence,

dead will live,

peace will prevail,

righteousness will rule ...

and this old scarred, polluted, gouged, abused planet will be restored to pristine beauty and harmony! Because the Creator who became our Savior rose up from the dead, ascended into heaven, was seated at the right hand of God the Father as King

---

2. Used by permission.
3. John 14:3.
4. Acts 1:10 – 11.

of Kings and Lord of Lords with all authority in the universe placed beneath His feet ... and He's coming back! One day, the sky will unfold, and Jesus will appear in clouds of glory to reign and rule in this world![5] Even His enemies will see Him and bow before Him.[6]

So open your eyes! Learn to tell time! And join me on the tiptoes of anticipation! He's coming! *I'm expecting to see Jesus!*[7] It's time to *wake up* ...!

Special Format for This Session

Your first group session will feature Anne's video message based on Matthew 24, in which she shares the signs Jesus gave His disciples to indicate the end of human history as we have known it.

Following the video and your group's discussion, you'll have opportunity to work at home on a personal Bible study using the guided questions provided on pages 16 – 22. These questions will help you search the Scriptures for yourself on this subject. Each of us needs to make up our own minds about the times in which we live, but our conclusion should be based not on what we think or feel or hope or want, but on the Word of God.

In the next session, Anne will share a simple exercise that will teach you how to listen for God's voice speak to you personally as you read your Bible.

---

5. Matthew 26:64.

6. Revelation 1:7; Philippians 2:9 – 11.

7. I believe that if I live out my natural lifetime, I will live to see the physical return of Jesus to earth. I base this on the signs that Jesus gave and how I see them being fulfilled in my generation. However, I readily admit that I may be mistaken. BUT I am still expecting to see Jesus, if not at His return, at my death!

Session 1 DVD Viewing Notes

As you watch the video presentation, use this section to take notes.

Learn how to tell time: What signs are we seeing take place in . . .

The religious realm?

The national realm?

The environmental realm?

The cultural realm?

The global realm?

Live by His clock: In light of what time it is, what are some practical ways you should . . .

Watch?

Work?

Walk?

Session 1 Small Group Discussion

1. Having considered the signs Jesus gave, and what you see taking place in our world today, what time do you think it is? Be prepared to explain your answer.

2. Select *one* of the following areas. How would knowing Jesus was coming tomorrow impact your life today?

   • Your attitudes or ambitions

   • Your decisions or dreams

   • Your family or friendships

   • Your priorities or prayers

- Your witness or your worship

- The way you spend your free time or money

3. If you knew Jesus were returning tomorrow, what things would you stop worrying about today? What things would you start worrying about?

Personal Bible Study

Knowing how to tell time becomes critically important for the child of God because we need to live with eternity in view. In other words, if you knew for sure that Jesus was going to return tomorrow, what would you do differently today? I want to live in that difference, 24/7, for the rest of my life. Because, dear reader, Jesus *is* coming! I'm expecting to see Jesus, either at His return or at my death! And when I do, I want to have as few regrets as possible.

To help you tell time, I have divided the signs into five categories. Through your Bible study time this week, become familiar with them so that you, too, learn to live by His clock.

DAY 1

Spiritual Signs

1. What warning did Jesus give in Matthew 24:4? How many times does He refer to this danger in this chapter? Give the phrases and verse numbers for each.

2. Give the phrase that repeats this warning in 2 Thessalonians 2:3.

3. Give some practical examples of how people today — especially the religious — are being deceived in regard to the end of the world and the coming of Christ.

4. From Matthew 24:5 – 12, give at least five signs in the spiritual or religious world, what each one means, and a contemporary example of each.

National Signs

1. What are two of the signs Jesus gave in the world of nations, from Matthew 24:6 – 7?

2. What is another national sign from Luke 21:25?

3. Give examples of these signs being fulfilled in our world today.

Environmental Signs

1. Give signs from the world of nature in Matthew 24:7; Luke 21:11; 21:25.

2. List examples of these signs that have occurred in our world during the past year.

DAY 2

Personal or Cultural Signs

1. What happened in Noah's day? See Genesis 6:5 – 14; 7:11 – 12, 17 – 23 for your answer.

2. Is there anything wrong with eating and drinking, marrying and giving in marriage, from Matthew 24:38? What was the real problem with Noah's generation?

3. How does Peter use this same analogy in 2 Peter 3:6?

4. What similarities do you see between Noah's generation and ours?

5. What are some other signs in the personal world from James 5:3 and 2 Timothy 3:1 – 5? Give examples of each.

Global Signs

1. From Matthew 24:14, what is perhaps the most exciting sign of all?

2. How is this sign uniquely being fulfilled in this generation?

3. What are you doing to help bring this to pass?

DAY 3

Watch

1. What do think Jesus means by "keep watch" in Matthew 24:42?

2. Why is this important, according to Matthew 24:42 – 44?

3. What are some practical things you can do in order to "keep watch"?

Work

1. From Matthew 24:45 – 47, what does Jesus want to find you and me doing when He returns?

2. If He returns in the next five minutes, what will He find you doing? What will you wish you had done?

3. Would you take a moment now to ask Him to give you a work assignment —
   something you can do that will make an eternal difference in the kingdom of
   God? Write His answer here.

DAY 4

Walk

1. When I walk with a friend or family member, we have to walk at the same pace
   and in the same direction or we can't walk together. Apply these two principles
   to walking with God.

2. Describe a walk that is pleasing to God from Ephesians 4:1 – 3. How does your
   walk compare?

3. What are some practical things you can do to adjust your walk to keep pace with
   His?

4. What does Jesus *not* want to find us doing, according to Matthew 24:48 – 51?

5. What are several things we are to do, in light of the imminent return of Christ, from 1 Peter 4:7?

From 2 Peter 3:11 – 12, 14, 17–18?

From 1 Thessalonians 4:11 – 12?

6. How does the hope of the return of Christ impact our lives so that we are motivated to get ready to see Jesus, according to 1 John 3:3? Can you give an example of this impact from your own life?

Wrapping Up

The Old Testament story of Noah illustrates the strategic necessity of a vibrant relationship with God. Noah was a man who lived at the end of his world as he had known it. He was facing the total annihilation of planet Earth. The flood that came was the equivalent of a nuclear meltdown. But Noah walked with God. As he did so, God told Noah that judgment was coming on the whole earth, and then gave Noah specific instructions on how to get ready so that he and his family would be saved from it.

It's a very sobering thought to realize what would have happened had Noah said he was too busy, too tired, too poor, too uneducated, too old to walk with God and then work for Him. If he had used any excuse at all for disobeying God ... or if he simply had not heard what God had to say ... you and I wouldn't be here today.

If the end of our world is coming ... or if the end of your world is coming through death or disease or disaster or divorce or some other devastating bend in the road or "abyss" that suddenly opens up beneath you ... the most vitally important thing you and I can do is to walk with God, listening to His voice, obeying His instructions. God will give us insight and wisdom so that not only will we know how to deal with whatever it is, but we can be used of God to help others also. Learn to live every day of your life expecting to see Jesus.

Listening for His Voice: Bible Study Workshop

This Bible study workshop has a single purpose: to present an approach that will help you know God in a personal relationship and communicate with Him through His Word as you learn to listen to His voice. The following information is introduced in detail in the video presentation. Use this section of the participant's guide as your viewing guide and workshop material. Underline key thoughts and take additional notes as you participate in the workshop. (The passage used as the example in the video workshop is on pages 28 – 29; a sample of a completed study is on pages 30 – 31.)

What You Need for Bible Study

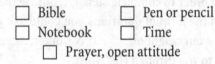

☐ Bible   ☐ Pen or pencil
☐ Notebook   ☐ Time
☐ Prayer, open attitude

⌐⌐

Steps to Bible Study

STEP 1: **Read God's Word.**
Begin by reading the designated passage of Scripture printed in each session which is divided into days (if your group meets less frequently than once a week, you may want to extend your study time for each passage). When you have finished reading the daily passage, move on to step 2.

STEP 2: **What does God's Word say?** *(List the facts.)*
When you have finished reading the passage, make a verse-by-verse list of the outstanding facts. Don't get caught up in the details; just pinpoint the most obvious facts. Ask yourself: Who is speaking? What is the subject? Where is it taking place? When did it happen? As you make your list, do not paraphrase, but use actual words from the passage itself.

STEP 3: **What does God's Word mean?** *(Learn the lessons.)*
After reading the passage and listing the facts, look for a lesson to learn from each fact. Ask yourself: What are the people in the passage doing that I should be doing? Is there a command I should obey? A promise I should claim? A warning I should heed? An example I should follow? Focus on spiritual lessons.

STEP 4: **What does God's Word mean to me?** *(Listen to His voice.)*
Though step 4 is the most meaningful, you can't do it effectively until you complete the first three steps. In order to complete step 4, rephrase the lessons you found in step 3 and put them in the form of questions you could ask yourself, your spouse, your child, your friend, your neighbor, or your coworker. As you write the questions, listen for God to speak to you through His Word.

There are some challenging passages in this study. Don't get hung up on what you don't understand. Look for the general principles and lessons that you can understand. The introduction prior to the passages in sessions 2–8, as well as the examples offered in steps 2, 3, and 4 of this session, will help you get started.

Remember, don't rush. It may take you several moments of prayerful meditation to discover meaningful lessons and hear God speaking to you. The object is not to get through it, but to develop a vibrant personal relationship with God.

STEP 5: How will I respond to God's Word? *(Live it out!)*
Read the assigned Scripture passages prayerfully, objectively, thoughtfully, and attentively as you listen for God to speak. He may not speak to you through every verse, but He *will* speak. When He does, record in the step 5 column the verse number (if applicable), what it is He seems to be saying to you, and your response to Him. You might like to date it as a means not only of keeping a spiritual journal, but also of holding yourself accountable to following through in obedience. God bless you as you seek to learn this simple yet effective method of reading His Word, that you might hear His voice speaking to you personally through it.

Read God's Word.
Mark 9:2 - 8

v.2 After six days Jesus took Peter, James
    and John with him and led them up
    a high mountain, where they were
    all alone. There he was transfigured
    before them.

v.3 His clothes became dazzling white,
    whiter than anyone in the world could
    bleach them.

v.4 And there appeared before them
    Elijah and Moses, who were talking
    with Jesus.

v.5 Peter said to Jesus, "Rabbi, it is good
    for us to be here. Let us put up three
    shelters — one for you, one for Moses
    and one for Elijah."

v.6 (He did not know what to say, they
    were so frightened.)

v.7 Then a cloud appeared and enveloped
    them, and a voice came from the
    cloud: "This is my Son, whom I love.
    Listen to him!"

v.8 Suddenly, when they looked around,
    they no longer saw anyone with them
    except Jesus.

What does God's Word say?
List the facts.

What does God's Word mean?
Learn the lessons.

What does God's Word mean to me?
Listen to His voice.

How will I respond to God's Word?
Live it out!

COMPLETED EXAMPLE

STEP 1	STEP 2

Read God's Word.
Mark 9:2 – 8

v.2 After six days Jesus took Peter, James and John with him and led them up a high mountain, where they were all alone. There he was transfigured before them.

v.3 His clothes became dazzling white, whiter than anyone in the world could bleach them.

v.4 And there appeared before them Elijah and Moses, who were talking with Jesus.

v.5 Peter said to Jesus, "Rabbi, it is good for us to be here. Let us put up three shelters — one for you, one for Moses and one for Elijah."

v.6 (He did not know what to say, they were so frightened.)

v.7 Then a cloud appeared and enveloped them, and a voice came from the cloud: "This is my Son, whom I love. Listen to him!"

v.8 Suddenly, when they looked around, they no longer saw anyone with them except Jesus.

What does God's Word say?
List the facts.

v.2 Jesus led Peter, James, and John alone up a mountain where he was transfigured.

v.3 His clothes became dazzling white.

v.4 Moses and Elijah appeared.

v.5 Peter said, "Let us put up three shelters."

v.6 He didn't know what to say.

v.7 A voice spoke from the cloud saying to listen to My Son.

v.8 Suddenly they no longer saw anyone but Jesus.

STEP 3

What does God's Word mean?
Learn the lessons.

v.2 We need to get away with Jesus —
He wants to be alone with us.

v.3 When we are alone, He reveals
Himself to us in fresh ways —
we have a fresh vision of who He is —
His glory.

v.4 Jesus is the focus of history —
and eternity.

v.5 Sometimes we want to stay on the
mountain.

v.6 If we don't know what to say, it's best
to say nothing.

v.7 God speaks to us — commands us to
listen to Jesus.

v.8 When everything passes away, there
will still be Jesus.

STEP 4

What does God's Word mean to me?
Listen to His voice.

v.2 When do I make time to get alone
with Jesus?

v.3 What fresh revelation of Jesus do I
have because I make time for Him?

v.4 What is my attitude toward the Old
Testament? Where is my focus?

v.5 Why am I reluctant to go back to the
valley?

v.6 When have I spoken when I should
have been silent?

v.7 Will I be obedient to God's command
and make the time to listen to His
voice?

v.8 How am I investing in that which will
last?

STEP 5

How will I respond to God's Word?
Live it out!

As I begin this study, I need to commit to regular time alone with the Lord, listening for
His voice to speak to me through His Word.

Wrapping Up

Now that you've had a chance to practice this method, use it! Pick your favorite passage from the Bible and try answering the questions (Steps 2 – 5) to unlock new meaning from the Scripture for your life. Enjoy the thrill of hearing God speak to you! Personally!

Preparing for the Next Session

First, read 2 Chronicles 34 in one sitting for the overview of the Scripture to be discussed in session 3. Then, in the time prior to your meeting, complete the four daily Bible study portions on pages 34 – 41. As you do, be prepared for what God will do as He reminds you and me that many of us are sleeping! It's time to begin the process of personal revival!

~ SESSION THREE ~

You're Sleeping!

History shows us what can happen when a civilization turns its back on God—and it also shows us the extraordinary changes that can happen when a fresh knowledge of God is sought after and reincorporated into a culture's priorities.

Expecting to See Jesus, p. 66–67

In 621 BC, the nation of Judah was spiritually asleep. A previous wicked king, Manasseh, had all but obliterated God from the people's thinking. Idolatry and child sacrifice were rampant, mimicking the religious practices of the neighboring pagan nations.

To make matters worse, the powerful kingdom of Babylon, east of Jerusalem, was threatening war and was crouching at Judah's doorstep.

If there ever was a nation that needed a wake-up call, it was Judah. That call came in a most surprising way ... as a result of a young man, Josiah, who had an experience of personal revival.

Josiah was only eight years old when he assumed the throne in Judah. His grandfather had been the wicked King Manasseh. When his father was assassinated in a conspiracy, Josiah found himself faced with the challenge of leading a nation that was provoking God's judgment. What a challenge!

In the midst of overwhelming obstacles, Josiah began to seek after God. At the young age of twenty, he led Judah in a powerful spiritual reformation as he tore down the altars and smashed the idols of the false religions that had permeated his nation. But it wasn't until he was twenty-six years old that he "saw the Lord," and experienced personal revival. And the revival began when God's Word was "found."

My prayer for you is that as you "find" God's Word on the following pages, you too will wake up to an experience of personal revival.

Personal Pre-Session Bible Study

By now you should have read 2 Chronicles 34 and completed the four Bible study worksheets on pages 34–41, assigned at the close of session 2. You'll review the personal applications in your group session and then hear from Anne on DVD as she and her guests discuss its relevance to your life.

DAY 1

Read God's Word.
2 Chronicles 34:1 – 5

v.1 Josiah was eight years old when he became king, and he reigned in Jerusalem thirty-one years.

v.2 He did what was right in the eyes of the LORD and walked in the ways of his father David, not turning aside to the right or to the left.

v.3 In the eighth year of his reign, while he was still young, he began to seek the God of his father David. In his twelfth year he began to purge Judah and Jerusalem of high places, Asherah poles, carved idols and cast images.

v.4 Under his direction the altars of the Baals were torn down; he cut to pieces the incense altars that were above them, and smashed the Asherah poles, the idols and the images. These he broke to pieces and scattered over the graves of those who had sacrificed to them.

v.5 He burned the bones of the priests on their altars, and so he purged Judah and Jerusalem.

What does God's Word say?
List the facts.

34

STEP 3

What does God's Word mean?
Learn the lessons.

STEP 4

What does God's Word mean to me?
Listen to His voice.

STEP 5

How will I respond to God's Word?
Live it out!

DAY 2

Read God's Word.
2 Chronicles 34:8 – 9, 14 – 15

v.8   In the eighteenth year of Josiah's reign, to purify the land and the temple, he sent Shaphan son of Azaliah and Maaseiah the ruler of the city, with Joah son of Joahaz, the recorder, to repair the temple of the LORD his God.

v.9   They went to Hilkiah the high priest and gave him the money that had been brought into the temple of God, which the Levites who were the doorkeepers had collected from the people....

v.14 While they were bringing out the money that had been taken into the temple of the LORD, Hilkiah the priest found the Book of the Law of the LORD that had been given through Moses.

v.15 Hilkiah said to Shaphan the secretary, "I have found the Book of the Law in the temple of the LORD." He gave it to Shaphan.

What does God's Word say?
List the facts.

36

STEP 3	STEP 4

What does God's Word mean?
Learn the lessons.

What does God's Word mean to me?
Listen to His voice.

STEP 5

How will I respond to God's Word?
Live it out!

DAY 3

Read God's Word.
2 Chronicles 34:29 – 31

v.29 Then the king called together all the elders of Judah and Jerusalem.

v.30 He went up to the temple of the LORD with the men of Judah, the people of Jerusalem, the priests and the Levites — all the people from the least to the greatest. He read in their hearing all the words of the Book of the Covenant, which had been found in the temple of the LORD.

v.31 The king stood by his pillar and renewed the covenant in the presence of the LORD — to follow the LORD and keep his commands, regulations and decrees with all his heart and all his soul, and to obey the words of the covenant written in this book.

What does God's Word say?
List the facts.

STEP 3

What does God's Word mean?
Learn the lessons.

STEP 4

What does God's Word mean to me?
Listen to His voice.

STEP 5

How will I respond to God's Word?
Live it out!

39

DAY 4

Read God's Word.
2 Chronicles 34:32 – 33

v.32 Then he had everyone in Jerusalem
and Benjamin pledge themselves to
it; the people of Jerusalem did this in
accordance with the covenant of God,
the God of their fathers.

v.33 Josiah removed all the detestable idols
from all the territory belonging to the
Israelites, and he had all who were
present in Israel serve the LORD their
God. As long as he lived, they did
not fail to follow the LORD, the God of
their fathers.

What does God's Word say?
List the facts.

What does God's Word mean?
Learn the lessons.

What does God's Word mean to me?
Listen to His voice.

How will I respond to God's Word?
Live it out!

Session 3 DVD Viewing Notes

As you watch the video presentation, use this section to take notes.

The state of the church: How did we get to this place?

The symptoms of sleep: When does service get in the way of a relationship with the Lord?

The start of revival: How do I begin the process of seeing the Lord?

Session 3 Small Group Discussion

1. Have you ever fallen asleep in your personal relationship with God? How do you think you got there?

2. Do you feel that you have role models who exemplify a vibrant personal relationship with God? If so, who are they?

3. What work are you doing for God which could be a distraction? Is this activity bringing you into a deeper relationship with God?

4. Describe a specific time or two when you felt that God was calling you to wake up.

5. How did you respond to those wake-up calls?

Wrapping Up

Do you sometimes look at other Christians whose faith seems so vibrantly alive and wonder what they have that you don't? Are you somewhat resentful of the way they speak so personally about God, as though they actually know Him intimately? Deep down within, do you yearn for more in your relationship with Him, yet you don't know how to get it or even what to ask for? You know God—and yet *you know something is missing!*

In order to find what's missing ... you need personal revival.

And personal revival is something that is impossible for you to do on your own because it involves a quiet, miraculous, eye-opening revelation of Him within your spirit.

You need to see the Lord.

Expecting to See Jesus, p. 84

As you look at the church and your own life, don't be discouraged. Once you realize you are asleep, you can make yourself available for the Holy Spirit to quicken you — to literally wake you up!

Preparing for the Next Session

In our next session, we will begin to see how God may use storms to wake us up to begin the journey of revival.

To prepare for session 4, please read Ezekiel 1:1 – 2:3 in one sitting for an overview of the Scripture to be discussed. Then, in the time prior to your meeting, complete the four daily Bible study portions on pages 48 – 55.

Wake Up!

In moments of despair, remember that God has allowed the crisis, and you and I need to be watchful for His message within the life-storm. It just might be our wake-up call.

Expecting to See Jesus, p. 88

When Jerusalem was captured in 597 BC, Ezekiel was forced to make the long trek across the desert to exile in Babylon. Although he spent the first twenty-five years of his life training for the priesthood in Jerusalem, he found himself the captive of a refugee camp. How his heart must have longed to serve God in the temple. How his heart must have struggled with his destroyed dreams. How he must have cried out for God to make sense of the senseless.

God heard the silent cry of Ezekiel's heart and gave him a breathtaking vision of His glory. Surrounded by the hopelessness and helplessness of the refugee camp, Ezekiel saw the Lord! He experienced personal revival.

As a result, Ezekiel ministered in a powerful way not as a priest, but as a prophet, to God's people in exile who desperately needed a word from the Lord. They were rebelling against God. Their nation and king gone, their beloved city of Jerusalem destroyed, their spectacular temple a pile of rubble, they were like a valley of dry bones — scattered in pieces with no life or form or function.

As the Lord awakened Ezekiel's heart to personal revival, God used Ezekiel to bring hope to the hopeless and life to the lifeless.

Through Ezekiel, God promised the nation would be reborn. Through Ezekiel and the people's extreme situation, God woke up the hearts of His people.

Open your eyes to the vision God gave to Ezekiel — can you hear God calling your heart to wake up to personal revival?

Personal Pre-Session Bible Study

By now you should have read Ezekiel 1:1 – 2:3 and completed the four Bible study worksheets on pages 48 – 55, assigned at the close of session 3. You'll review the personal applications in your group session and then hear from Anne on DVD as she and her guests discuss its relevance to your life.

DAY 1

Read God's Word.
Ezekiel 1:1 – 3

v.1   In the thirtieth year, in the fourth month on the fifth day, while I was among the exiles by the Kebar River, the heavens were opened and I saw visions of God.

v.2   On the fifth of the month — it was the fifth year of the exile of King Jehoiachin —

v.3   the word of the LORD came to Ezekiel the priest, the son of Buzi, by the Kebar River in the land of the Babylonians. There the hand of the LORD was upon him.

What does God's Word say?
List the facts.

What does God's Word mean?
Learn the lessons.

What does God's Word mean to me?
Listen to His voice.

How will I respond to God's Word?
Live it out!

DAY 2

| STEP 1 | STEP 2 |

Read God's Word.
Ezekiel 1:4 – 5, 24

v.4   I looked, and I saw a windstorm coming out of the north — an immense cloud with flashing lightning and surrounded by brilliant light. The center of the fire looked like glowing metal,

v.5   and in the fire was what looked like four living creatures. In appearance their form was that of a man, ...

v.24 When the creatures moved, I heard the sound of their wings, like the roar of rushing waters, like the voice of the Almighty, like the tumult of an army. When they stood still, they lowered their wings.

What does God's Word say?
List the facts.

STEP 3

What does God's Word mean?
Learn the lessons.

STEP 4

What does God's Word mean to me?
Listen to His voice.

STEP 5

How will I respond to God's Word?
Live it out!

51

DAY 3

Read God's Word.
Ezekiel 1:25 – 28

What does God's Word say?
List the facts.

v.25 Then there came a voice from above the expanse over their heads as they stood with lowered wings.

v.26 Above the expanse over their heads was what looked like a throne of sapphire, and high above on the throne was a figure like that of a man.

v.27 I saw that from what appeared to be his waist up he looked like glowing metal, as if full of fire, and that from there down he looked like fire; and brilliant light surrounded him.

v.28 Like the appearance of a rainbow in the clouds on a rainy day, so was the radiance around him. This was the appearance of the likeness of the glory of the LORD. When I saw it, I fell facedown, and I heard the voice of one speaking.

What does God's Word mean?
Learn the lessons.

What does God's Word mean to me?
Listen to His voice.

How will I respond to God's Word?
Live it out!

DAY 4

Read God's Word.
Ezekiel 2:1 – 3

v.1 He said to me, "Son of man, stand up on your feet and I will speak to you."

v.2 As he spoke, the Spirit came into me and raised me to my feet, and I heard him speaking to me.

v.3 He said: "Son of man, I am sending you to the Israelites, to a rebellious nation that has rebelled against me; they and their fathers have been in revolt against me to this very day."

What does God's Word say?
List the facts.

What does God's Word mean?
Learn the lessons.

What does God's Word mean to me?
Listen to His voice.

How will I respond to God's Word?
Live it out!

Session 4 DVD Viewing Notes

As you watch the video presentation, use this section to take notes.

Powerful storms: Why does God use storms to speak?

Personal storms: What are the storms in your life?

Pointed storms: How do you make sure you get the message?

Session 4 Small Group Discussion

1. Why does God use storms to speak to us?

2. Name specific storms in your life that may not have made headlines. What was God trying to tell you?

3. Out of what comfort zone is God calling you?

4. What shelter do you look for in your storm?

5. How can you make sure that you don't miss the message in the storm?

Wrapping Up

When disaster strikes, whether it's national, such as a destructive hurricane or the 9/11 attack on America; or personal, such as divorce, death, or disease; or economic, such as a job layoff or a stock market crash or recession; or any other mortal, emotional, or financial storm, it's critical that you and I look up! Don't miss the message! *God may be calling....*

If your life is being shaken, get ready for what very well may be a life-changing experience of personal revival. This may be the very wake-up call God uses to open your eyes to the vision of His glory.

Expecting to See Jesus, pp. 98-99

Have hope! God uses storms in your life to get your attention. If you begin to see beyond your own despair, then you can rest assured that His Holy Spirit is already at work and performing a good work in your life. He is waking you from your sleep.

Preparing for the Next Session

In our next session, we will begin to see what God is showing us once He has opened our eyes, and what it means to behold the glory of the Lord.

To prepare for session 5, please read Exodus 33 – 34 in one sitting for an overview of the Scripture to be discussed. Then, in the time prior to your meeting, complete the four daily Bible study portions on pages 62 – 69.

Open Your Eyes!

There is one true, living God who created all things and who controls all things — a God who has chosen to reveal Himself to you and to me. We just need to ... open our eyes to Him.... And the eyes that need to be opened are not the eyes in our head, but the eyes of our heart.

Expecting to See Jesus, p. 106

God had delivered His children from bondage in Egypt with a titanic display of His power. He had parted the Red Sea enabling them to cross on dry ground, He had supernaturally destroyed the pursuing army of Pharaoh, and He had daily fed them with manna.

But the Israelites still lacked complete trust in God. They complained, murmured, and whined every step of the journey as Moses sought to lead them to the Promised Land. As the people's discontent grew, they even built a golden calf to worship and spoke of returning to Egypt. They questioned and challenged Moses' leadership.

Moses was desperate! If ever someone needed a fresh touch from God, Moses did! And so he deliberately, intentionally sought out God. He asked for an experience of personal revival. He asked God to show him His glory! And God did! *Moses saw the Lord!*

Moses recorded all that God said to him, then returned to lead the people with renewed passion, vision, and energy.

As Moses reentered the camp of Israel after having seen the Lord, the Israelites could see a visible change in their leader. His face was radiant as it reflected God's glory. Moses was not only spiritually revived, but even his physical appearance was transformed from the encounter with God.

Ask God to show you His glory! Open your eyes to Him! I wonder: What spiritual and physical changes will take place in your life today as a result?

Personal Pre-Session Bible Study

By now you should have read Exodus 33 – 34 and completed the four Bible study worksheets on pages 62 – 69, assigned at the close of session 4. You'll review the personal applications in your group session and then hear from Anne on DVD as she and her guests discuss its relevance to your life.

DAY 1

Read God's Word.
Exodus 33:12 – 14

v.12 Moses said to the Lord, "You have
been telling me, 'Lead these people,'
but you have not let me know whom
you will send with me. You have said,
'I know you by name and you have
found favor with me.'

v.13 If you are pleased with me, teach
me your ways so I may know you
and continue to find favor with you.
Remember that this nation is your
people."

v.14 The Lord replied, "My Presence will
go with you, and I will give you rest."

What does God's Word say?
List the facts.

STEP 3

What does God's Word mean?
Learn the lessons.

STEP 4

What does God's Word mean to me?
Listen to His voice.

STEP 5

How will I respond to God's Word?
Live it out!

DAY 2

Read God's Word.
Exodus 33:15 – 17

v.15 Then Moses said to him, "If your Presence does not go with us, do not send us up from here.

v.16 How will anyone know that you are pleased with me and with your people unless you go with us? What else will distinguish me and your people from all the other people on the face of the earth?"

v.17 And the LORD said to Moses, "I will do the very thing you have asked, because I am pleased with you and I know you by name."

What does God's Word say?
List the facts.

STEP 3	STEP 4
What does God's Word mean? *Learn the lessons.*	*What does God's Word mean to me?* *Listen to His voice.*

STEP 5

How will I respond to God's Word?
Live it out!

DAY 3

Read God's Word.
Exodus 33:18 – 23

v.18 Then Moses said, "Now show me your glory."

v.19 And the LORD said, "I will cause all my goodness to pass in front of you, and I will proclaim my name, the LORD, in your presence. I will have mercy on whom I will have mercy, and I will have compassion on whom I will have compassion.

v.20 But," he said, "you cannot see my face, for no one may see me and live."

v.21 Then the LORD said, "There is a place near me where you may stand on a rock.

v.22 When my glory passes by, I will put you in a cleft in the rock and cover you with my hand until I have passed by.

v.23 Then I will remove my hand and you will see my back; but my face must not be seen."

What does God's Word say?
List the facts.

What does God's Word mean?
Learn the lessons.

What does God's Word mean to me?
Listen to His voice.

How will I respond to God's Word?
Live it out!

DAY 4

Read God's Word.
Exodus 34:29 – 32

v.29   When Moses came down from
Mount Sinai with the two tablets of
the Testimony in his hands, he was
not aware that his face was radiant
because he had spoken with the LORD.

v.30   When Aaron and all the Israelites saw
Moses, his face was radiant, and they
were afraid to come near him.

v.31   But Moses called to them; so Aaron
and all the leaders of the community
came back to him, and he spoke to
them.

v.32   Afterward all the Israelites came
near him, and he gave them all the
commands the LORD had given him on
Mount Sinai.

What does God's Word say?
List the facts.

What does God's Word mean?
Learn the lessons.

What does God's Word mean to me?
Listen to His voice.

How will I respond to God's Word?
Live it out!

Session 5 DVD Viewing Notes

As you watch the video presentation, use this section to take notes.

The radiance of God's glory: What are we asking for when we ask to see God's glory?

The revelation of God's glory: What have you learned of God's character? How did you learn it?

The result of God's glory: What should your life look like after you've experienced God's glory?

Session 5 Small Group Discussion

1. Have you ever asked God to show you His glory? What was revealed to you?

2. What characteristic of God has He revealed to you recently that you did not know before?

3. When has God tried to reveal Himself to you that you were not able to see or hear Him? Why?

4. During what circumstances has your knowledge of God deepened? When has He drawn you closer to Himself?

Wrapping Up

Is God trying to pry open the eyes of your heart so He can show you His glory? Is He using a personal, emotional, or financial life-shaking experience you are enduring for that purpose? And have you misunderstood so that, the more intense your situation becomes, the more tightly you squeeze your eyes shut against Him and what He is trying to reveal to you?

Stop resisting him. Stop resenting Him. Stop complaining. Stop feeling sorry for yourself. Stop demanding what you want.... Adjust your attitude. Change your mind about things—about yourself—about others—about Him. Relax in total trust. He knows what He's doing.... Let go, and look up! Let Him open the eyes of your heart. OPEN YOUR EYES! *Open your eyes* to the vision of His glory! Prayerfully, expectantly, sincerely, open your eyes to Him!

Expecting to See Jesus, pp. 107 - 108

Glimpsing the glory of the Lord is a penetrating, expanding, life-deepening, life-enriching experience. Don't resist Him because of the storm. Open the eyes of your heart to see Him in a fresh way.

Preparing for the Next Session

In our next session, we will discover where God's glory leads us and what it truly means to be burdened by our sin: to rend our hearts.

To prepare for session 6, please read 2 Samuel 12 and Psalm 51 in one sitting for an overview of the Scripture to be discussed. Then, in the time prior to your meeting, complete the four daily Bible study portions on pages 76 – 83.

Rend Your Heart!

> Think back in your life. When have you felt the acute weight and unshakable burden of your sin?... Could it be, dear one, that that was your encounter with the spotless, sinless Son of God? Could it be that the nearer to Him you actually are, the closer to hell you actually feel because your sin becomes glaringly apparent in the searing light of His holiness? Could it be that God is calling you to "rend your heart"?
>
> *Expecting to See Jesus*, pp. 138–139

David was a man after God's own heart. But David was a sinner like you and I, vulnerable in ease and comfort. From his rooftop one evening, David saw his neighbor's wife, Bathsheba, bathing. His desire was aroused and he sent for her, taking her as his lover. While David chose his sin, he could not choose sin's consequences. And sin always has consequences.

Bathsheba became pregnant with David's child. To hide his adultery, David ordered Bathsheba's husband, Uriah, a soldier fighting David's battles, into the front lines. David knew this order was a death sentence.

Upon Uriah's death, David was guilty not only of adultery and lying, but murder. David's scheme almost worked. He married Bathsheba. He appeared happy and oblivious to the sin in his life, but God refused to let David live in such serious spiritual denial. He sent the prophet Nathan to speak His Word into David's life. The penetrating conviction that came from the scorching personal application of God's Word caused David to rend his heart in humble contrition. He poured out his confession of sin in one of the most moving prayers in Scripture.

What sin have you committed of which you are unaware? How have you provoked God's displeasure? What is hindering you from receiving the fullness of His blessing? What sin is quenching the fire of revival in your heart? It's time to rend your heart! Pray David's prayer of confession as your own, asking God to have mercy and blot out your transgressions as you name them one by one.

Personal Pre-Session Bible Study

By now you should have read 2 Samuel 12 and Psalm 51 and completed the four Bible study worksheets on pages 76–83, assigned at the close of session 5. You'll review the personal applications in your group session and then hear from Anne on DVD as she and her guests discuss its relevance to your life.

DAY 1

Read God's Word.
Psalm 51:1 – 4

v.1 Have mercy on me, O God, according
to your unfailing love; according to
your great compassion blot out my
transgressions.

v.2 Wash away all my iniquity and
cleanse me from my sin.

v.3 For I know my transgressions, and
my sin is always before me.

v.4 Against you, you only, have I sinned
and done what is evil in your sight, so
that you are proved right when you
speak and justified when you judge.

What does God's Word say?
List the facts.

What does God's Word mean?
Learn the lessons.

What does God's Word mean to me?
Listen to His voice.

How will I respond to God's Word?
Live it out!

DAY 2

Read God's Word.
Psalm 51:5 - 9

v.5 Surely I was sinful at birth, sinful from the time my mother conceived me.

v.6 Surely you desire truth in the inner parts; you teach me wisdom in the inmost place.

v.7 Cleanse me with hyssop, and I will be clean; wash me, and I will be whiter than snow.

v.8 Let me hear joy and gladness; let the bones you have crushed rejoice.

v.9 Hide your face from my sins and blot out all my iniquity.

What does God's Word say?
List the facts.

What does God's Word mean?
Learn the lessons.

What does God's Word mean to me?
Listen to His voice.

How will I respond to God's Word?
Live it out!

DAY 3

Read God's Word.
Psalm 51:10 – 13

v.10 Create in me a pure heart, O God, and
renew a steadfast spirit within me.

v.11 Do not cast me from your presence or
take your Holy Spirit from me.

v.12 Restore to me the joy of your salvation
and grant me a willing spirit, to
sustain me.

v.13 Then I will teach transgressors your
ways, and sinners will turn back to
you.

What does God's Word say?
List the facts.

What does God's Word mean?
Learn the lessons.

What does God's Word mean to me?
Listen to His voice.

How will I respond to God's Word?
Live it out!

DAY 4

Read God's Word.
Psalm 51:14 – 17

v.14 Save me from bloodguilt, O God, the
God who saves me, and my tongue
will sing of your righteousness.

v.15 O Lord, open my lips, and my mouth
will declare your praise.

v.16 You do not delight in sacrifice, or
I would bring it; you do not take
pleasure in burnt offerings.

v.17 The sacrifices of God are a broken
spirit; a broken and contrite heart, O
God, you will not despise.

What does God's Word say?
List the facts.

What does God's Word mean?
Learn the lessons.

What does God's Word mean to me?
Listen to His voice.

How will I respond to God's Word?
Live it out!

Session 6 DVD Viewing Notes

As you watch the video presentation, use this section to take notes.

Seriousness of sin: How does sin prevent you from "seeing the Lord"?

Struggle with sin: When have you truly wrestled with the sin in your life?

Sorrow for sin: What is keeping you from dealing with sin?

Session 6 Small Group Discussion

1. How did David let his guard down?

   What things could lead you to let your guard down?

2. How have you seen the consequence of sin in your life or in the lives of those around you?

3. Describe a specific time that you have been tempted and how God provided a way out.

4. Have you ever been deceived by sin? How?

5. When have you felt devastated by sin? What do you think it means to truly rend your heart?

Wrapping Up

I hate sin, and I don't want to sin, but it's my nature to do it. And although I have victory over sin when I live in my new nature by the power of His Spirit, the sin I still commit makes me sick of myself. Sometimes the sin is not obvious, and for that reason, from time to time, I need a wake-up call to personal revival—a fresh experience and vision of Christ in order to open my eyes to His holiness and my helplessness and the eternal hope of the Cross. I need to come back to the Cross and get right with Him—not for forgiveness, since I am forgiven forever, but for sweet fellowship with Him and for power in His service.

Expecting to See Jesus, p. 146

Sin is deceptive and temptation always lurks at your doorstep. Like David, you too can be easy prey. But God does not leave you in your sin. Through his grace, you may experience the pain and burden of conviction and guilt, so that you may truly rend your heart.

Preparing for the Next Session

In our next session, we will begin to see how rending our hearts leads to authentic repentance and bending our knees before God.

To prepare for session 7, please read Ezra 7 – 10 in one sitting for an overview of the Scripture to be discussed. Then, in the time prior to your meeting, complete the four daily Bible study portions on pages 90 – 97.

Bend Your Knees!

> No one ... is exempt from the need to come to the Cross and be cleansed of sin. The level ground at the foot of the Cross leaves no room for self-righteousness or judgmentalness or a critical spirit or pride or self-promotion or hypocrisy. We are all helpless and hopeless in our sinful condition apart from the shed blood of Jesus Christ.
>
> *Expecting to See Jesus, p. 157*

God's children were held captive in Babylon for seventy years. Then, in 539 BC, Babylon was conquered by Persia. Cyrus, the Persian king, issued a decree that all of the Jews were free to return home to Jerusalem. He even offered his help to rebuild their demolished temple, ordering the Babylonians to give money, livestock, and return any treasured religious articles that had been looted.

Under Zerubbabel's leadership and encouraged by the prophets Zechariah and Haggai, a remnant of Jews returned to Jerusalem and rebuilt the temple.

Some time later, Ezra, a man who had devoted himself to studying, obeying, and teaching God's Word, led another group of exiles from Babylon to Jerusalem.

All seemed well as he entered the city. But on closer examination, he made a shocking discovery — God's people had lapsed back into serious sin and compromise with the world around them. Ezra's reaction was dramatic: he tore his coat, fell on his knees, wept, and poured out heartfelt shame before God for the sin of His people.

As Ezra prayed, confessing and weeping, a large crowd gathered around him. They too began to grieve and mourn for their sin. As a result of Ezra's wet eyes, bent knees, and broken heart, the people of God were led in national repentance and revival.

When was the last time you wept over sin? When has your heart been broken for that which breaks God's heart? When have you fallen on your knees in humble, sincere repentance? Who would be led to repentance and revival if you did?

Personal Pre-Session Bible Study

By now you should have read Ezra 7 – 10 and completed the four Bible study worksheets on pages 90 – 97, assigned at the close of session 6. You'll review the personal applications in your group session and then hear from Anne on DVD as she and her guests discuss its relevance to your life.

DAY 1

Read God's Word.
Ezra 7:6; 9:1 – 3

7:6   this Ezra came up from Babylon. He
        was a teacher well versed in the Law
        of Moses, which the LORD, the God of
        Israel, had given....

9:1   After these things had been done,
        the leaders came to me and said,
        "The people of Israel, including
        the priests and the Levites, have
        not kept themselves separate from
        the neighboring peoples with their
        detestable practices, like those of
        the Canaanites, Hittites, Perizzites,
        Jebusites, Ammonites, Moabites,
        Egyptians and Amorites.

v.2   They have taken some of their
        daughters as wives for themselves and
        their sons, and have mingled the holy
        race with the peoples around them.
        And the leaders and officials have led
        the way in this unfaithfulness."

v.3   When I heard this, I tore my tunic
        and cloak, pulled hair from my head
        and beard and sat down appalled.

What does God's Word say?
List the facts.

STEP 3

What does God's Word mean?
Learn the lessons.

STEP 4

What does God's Word mean to me?
Listen to His voice.

STEP 5

How will I respond to God's Word?
Live it out!

DAY 2

Read God's Word.
Ezra 9:4 – 7

What does God's Word say?
List the facts.

v.4   Then everyone who trembled at the words of the God of Israel gathered around me because of this unfaithfulness of the exiles. And I sat there appalled until the evening sacrifice.

v.5   Then, at the evening sacrifice, I rose from my self-abasement, with my tunic and cloak torn, and fell on my knees with my hands spread out to the LORD my God

v.6   and prayed: "O my God, I am too ashamed and disgraced to lift up my face to you, my God, because our sins are higher than our heads and our guilt has reached to the heavens.

v.7   From the days of our forefathers until now, our guilt has been great. Because of our sins, we and our kings and our priests have been subjected to the sword and captivity, to pillage and humiliation at the hand of foreign kings, as it is today."

STEP 3

What does God's Word mean?
Learn the lessons.

STEP 4

What does God's Word mean to me?
Listen to His voice.

STEP 5

How will I respond to God's Word?
Live it out!

DAY 3

Read God's Word.
Ezra 9:8 – 10

v.8 "But now, for a brief moment, the LORD our God has been gracious in leaving us a remnant and giving us a firm place in his sanctuary, and so our God gives light to our eyes and a little relief in our bondage.

v.9 Though we are slaves, our God has not deserted us in our bondage. He has shown us kindness in the sight of the kings of Persia: He has granted us new life to rebuild the house of our God and repair its ruins, and he has given us a wall of protection in Judah and Jerusalem.

v.10 But now, O our God, what can we say after this? For we have disregarded the commands..."

What does God's Word say?
List the facts.

What does God's Word mean?
Learn the lessons.

What does God's Word mean to me?
Listen to His voice.

How will I respond to God's Word?
Live it out!

DAY 4

Read God's Word.
Ezra 9:13, 15; 10:1

What does God's Word say?
List the facts.

9:13 "What has happened to us is a result
of our evil deeds and our great guilt,
and yet, our God, you have punished
us less than our sins have deserved
and have given us a remnant like this.

v.15 O Lord, God of Israel, you are
righteous! We are left this day as a
remnant. Here we are before you in
our guilt, though because of it not one
of us can stand in your presence."

10:1 While Ezra was praying and
confessing, weeping and
throwing himself down before
the house of God, a large crowd
of Israelites — men, women and
children — gathered around him.
They too wept bitterly.

What does God's Word mean?
Learn the lessons.

What does God's Word mean to me?
Listen to His voice.

How will I respond to God's Word?
Live it out!

Session 7 DVD Viewing Notes

As you watch the video presentation, use this section to take notes.

Recognition of sin: Why do we have trouble identifying sin?

Repentance of sin: How should we deal with the sin in our own lives? What difference does our attitude toward sin make in the lives of those around us?

Restoration after sin: How do we deal with the guilt of forgiven sin?

Session 7 Small Group Discussion

1. Like Ezra, when have you felt like you were a prisoner to your circumstances? How have you dealt with it?

2. How has the Holy Spirit convicted you of sin in your life?

3. Do you have leaders or mentors in your life who understand the seriousness of sin? How do they convey this to you?

4. In what ways does our culture lower the standards of God, like the Israelites living among the Canaanites?

5. What does true repentance look like? When have you wept over your sin or the sin around you?

6. How have you dealt with the guilt of sin in your life?

Wrapping Up

Every day, I bow in utter humility with a contrite heart that is filled with gratitude for the merciful, saving power of God, knowing with deep conviction that if He uses me in ministry it is purely by His grace alone. Because I'm just a desperate sinner, ruined and responsible for sin, but one who has been to the foot of the Cross.

Expecting to See Jesus, p. 157

On your knees, in tears of grief before the Lord, you can begin to understand and experience genuine repentance. Bend your knees before God.

Preparing for the Next Session

In our next session, we will learn where God will lead us after we have bent our knees before Him. How do we hear God's call in our life and what is our response to His compelling voice?

To prepare for session 8, please read Isaiah 6 in one sitting for an overview of the Scripture to be discussed. Then, in the time prior to your meeting, complete the daily Bible study portions on pages 104 – 109. Note that there are only three portions for session 8, not the usual four.

Just Say Yes!

> When our Shepherd speaks, He speaks to us personally—by name....
> He speaks in the language of our own personal lives.
> Will you say, "Yes, Lord. Here am I. Send me!"?
> *Expecting to See Jesus,* p. 171

In the year King Uzziah died, Isaiah saw the Lord. It has been suggested that Uzziah might have been Isaiah's relative. Therefore, the king's death created great ripples throughout Isaiah's life. His material comfort, protection, and emotions were all being shaken. However, this storm allowed Isaiah to be ready for all God had in store for him.

By being open to the Lord, Isaiah witnessed a direct manifestation of the Lord's glory through the stunning images of the seraphs proclaiming the holiness of the Lord.

In the presence of the Lord, Isaiah was convicted of his own sin. As he recognized his sin and rended his heart, he experienced full atonement in the presence of Almighty God. Think about it. Isaiah's experience represents every element of our journey to personal revival.

After seeing the Lord, Isaiah was ready for service. The voice of the Lord called out, "Whom shall I send? And who will go for us?"

I can imagine Isaiah's shaking hand slowly coming out from his cloak as a sign of his willingness to go. Then, he said the sweet words of commitment. "Here am I. Send me!"

Isaiah's vision catapulted him from the grief-tinged mundane to the heights of glory to the depths of sin to the foot of the Cross. The personal revival that Isaiah experienced compelled him to offer his life in service to the Lord. Are you ready to follow him? Then, just say yes.

Personal Pre-Session Bible Study

By now you should have read Isaiah 6 and completed the three (not the usual four) Bible study worksheets on pages 104–109, assigned at the close of session 7. You'll review the personal applications in your group session and then hear from Anne on DVD as she and her guests discuss its relevance to your life.

DAY 1

Read God's Word.
Isaiah 6:1 – 3

v.1 In the year that King Uzziah died, I saw the Lord seated on a throne, high and exalted, and the train of his robe filled the temple.

v.2 Above him were seraphs, each with six wings: With two wings they covered their faces, with two they covered their feet, and with two they were flying.

v.3 And they were calling to one another: "Holy, holy, holy is the LORD Almighty; the whole earth is full of his glory."

What does God's Word say?
List the facts.

STEP 3

What does God's Word mean?
Learn the lessons.

STEP 4

What does God's Word mean to me?
Listen to His voice.

STEP 5

How will I respond to God's Word?
Live it out!

DAY 2

Read God's Word.
Isaiah 6:4 – 5

v.4 At the sound of their voices the doorposts and thresholds shook and the temple was filled with smoke.

v.5 "Woe to me!" I cried. "I am ruined! For I am a man of unclean lips, and I live among a people of unclean lips, and my eyes have seen the King, the LORD Almighty."

What does God's Word say?
List the facts.

What does God's Word mean?
Learn the lessons.

What does God's Word mean to me?
Listen to His voice.

How will I respond to God's Word?
Live it out!

DAY 3

Read God's Word.
Isaiah 6:6 - 8

v.6 Then one of the seraphs flew to me
with a live coal in his hand, which he
had taken with tongs from the altar.

v.7 With it he touched my mouth and
said, "See, this has touched your lips;
your guilt is taken away and your sin
atoned for."

v.8 Then I heard the voice of the Lord
saying, "Whom shall I send? And who
will go for us?" And I said, "Here am
I. Send me!"

What does God's Word say?
List the facts.

STEP 3

What does God's Word mean?
Learn the lessons.

STEP 4

What does God's Word mean to me?
Listen to His voice.

STEP 5

How will I respond to God's Word?
Live it out!

Session 8 DVD Viewing Notes

As you watch the video presentation, use this section to take notes.

Hearing: How have you heard God's voice?

Hesitating: Has there been a time when you have heard God's voice, but struggled with heeding it?

Heeding: What happens when we just say yes?

Here am I: Five minutes before you die, what will you wish you had done differently?

Session 8 Small Group Discussion

1. How did God call Isaiah?

   How has God called you?

2. What excuses have you given God for not heeding His voice?

3. What are the areas in your life where you have stepped out to follow God? What are areas where you still need to step out?

4. What is the consequence of resisting God's call? What are the blessings of making yourself available for His service?

Wrapping Up

> One of the lasting impacts of personal revival is that it has made a difference in my life. I not only listen to the voice of Jesus and apply His words to my life, but I live for Him alone. I am so caught up in who He is and what He has done for me that I no longer consider my life my own. My life is laid down at His nail-pierced feet, totally available for His use. Anytime. Anywhere. Anyway. The supreme joy of my life is to be available to Him.
>
> *Expecting to See Jesus, p. 175*

When God calls you, you must respond. Isaiah did, and it changed his life forever. God will provide you with everything you need. When you hear the voice of the Father, just say yes!

Preparing for the Next Session

In our next session, we will discuss how God's call in our life motivates us forward into action.

To prepare for session 9, please read Nehemiah 1, 2, 6, and 8 in one sitting for an overview of the Scripture to be discussed. Then, in the time prior to your meeting, complete the four daily Bible study portions on pages 116 – 123.

Move Your Feet!

> You *cannot* experience personal revival in your relationship with Jesus Christ and *do nothing!* If you truly have awakened, opened your eyes, rended your heart, bent your knees, and said yes, then it naturally follows that you *must* move your feet!
>
> *Expecting to See Jesus*, p. 183

The remnant of the Jewish nation that returned to Judah from Babylon was demoralized. They had managed to rebuild the temple, but the walls of Jerusalem were still in rubble. They were open to attack and were becoming stagnant in their work to reconstruct their lives.

Nehemiah, a trusted personal servant of the Persian king, Artaxerxes, heard about the terrible conditions in Judah and grieved. When the king asked what was wrong, Nehemiah shared his heart's desire to go to Jerusalem and rebuild the wall. King Artaxerxes gave Nehemiah his blessing and resources to help.

After years of little or no progress, under Nehemiah's leadership God's people rebuilt Jerusalem's walls in fifty-two days. Nehemiah's efforts were blessed of God with amazing results. Following the rebuilding of the wall, Nehemiah was joined by Ezra, the great Bible teacher who had led the original exiles in revival years earlier. As Ezra read God's Word to God's people, they were deeply convicted of sin. Men moved throughout the crowd to explain what had been read, and to lead the people in confession and repentance. The people wept and mourned for their sin, then burst into the joy of sins forgiven as they experienced, once again, personal revival, recognizing God's presence in their midst.

The actions of both Ezra and Nehemiah, following God's directions, made a lasting impact on the lives of God's people, leading them to national security as well as national revival.

I wonder: What lasting impact will your actions have as you follow God's directions?

Personal Pre-Session Bible Study

By now you should have read Nehemiah 1, 2, 6, and 8 and completed the four Bible study worksheets on pages 116 – 123, assigned at the close of session 8. You'll review the personal applications in your group session and then hear from Anne on DVD as she and her guests discuss its relevance to your life.

DAY 1

Read God's Word.
Nehemiah 1:1 – 4

v.1   The words of Nehemiah son of
      Hacaliah: In the month of Kislev in
      the twentieth year, while I was in the
      citadel of Susa,

v.2   Hanani, one of my brothers, came
      from Judah with some other men, and
      I questioned them about the Jewish
      remnant that survived the exile, and
      also about Jerusalem.

v.3   They said to me, "Those who survived
      the exile and are back in the province
      are in great trouble and disgrace. The
      wall of Jerusalem is broken down, and
      its gates have been burned with fire."

v.4   When I heard these things, I sat down
      and wept. For some days I mourned
      and fasted and prayed before the God
      of heaven.

What does God's Word say?
List the facts.

116

STEP 3

What does God's Word mean?
Learn the lessons.

STEP 4

What does God's Word mean to me?
Listen to His voice.

STEP 5

How will I respond to God's Word?
Live it out!

DAY 2

STEP 1   STEP 2

Read God's Word.
Nehemiah 1:5 – 7, 11

v.5   Then I said: "O Lord, God of heaven,
the great and awesome God, who
keeps his covenant of love with
those who love him and obey his
commands,

v.6   let your ear be attentive and your
eyes open to hear the prayer your
servant is praying before you day and
night for your servants, the people of
Israel. I confess the sins we Israelites,
including myself and my father's
house, have committed against you.

v.7   We have acted very wickedly
toward you. We have not obeyed the
commands, decrees and laws you
gave your servant Moses.

v.11 O Lord, let your ear be attentive to the
prayer of this your servant and to the
prayer of your servants who delight
in revering your name. Give your
servant success today by granting
him favor in the presence of this
man." I was cupbearer to the king.

What does God's Word say?
List the facts.

STEP 3	STEP 4

What does God's Word mean?
Learn the lessons.

What does God's Word mean to me?
Listen to His voice.

STEP 5

How will I respond to God's Word?
Live it out!

DAY 3

Read God's Word.
Nehemiah 2:1 – 5

v.1 In the month of Nisan in the
twentieth year of King Artaxerxes,
when wine was brought for him, I
took the wine and gave it to the king.
I had not been sad in his presence
before;

v.2 so the king asked me, "Why does your
face look so sad when you are not ill?
This can be nothing but sadness of
heart." I was very much afraid,

v.3 but I said to the king, "May the king
live forever! Why should my face
not look sad when the city where my
fathers are buried lies in ruins, and its
gates have been destroyed by fire?"

v.4 The king said to me, "What is it you
want?" Then I prayed to the God of
heaven,

v.5 and I answered the king, "If it pleases
the king and if your servant has found
favor in his sight, let him send me to
the city in Judah where my fathers are
buried so that I can rebuild it."

What does God's Word say?
List the facts.

What does God's Word mean?
Learn the lessons.

What does God's Word mean to me?
Listen to His voice.

How will I respond to God's Word?
Live it out!

DAY 4

Read God's Word.
Nehemiah 2:6; 6:15 – 16

2:6 Then the king, with the queen sitting beside him, asked me, "How long will your journey take, and when will you get back?" It pleased the king to send me; so I set a time.

6:15 So the wall was completed on the twenty-fifth of Elul, in fifty-two days.

v.16 When all our enemies heard about this, all the surrounding nations were afraid and lost their self-confidence, because they realized that this work had been done with the help of our God.

What does God's Word say?
List the facts.

STEP 3	STEP 4
What does God's Word mean? *Learn the lessons.*	*What does God's Word mean to me?* *Listen to His voice.*

STEP 5

How will I respond to God's Word?
Live it out!

Session 9 Viewing Notes

As you watch the video presentation, use this section to take notes.

Pay attention: What need has grabbed your heart?

Pray: What part does prayer play in revival?

Put on the clothes of the call: How has God equipped you to serve Him? Have you obeyed?

Putting your faith into practice: What does God want to accomplish through you?

Session 9 Small Group Discussion

1. What burdens has God placed on your heart? How have you responded?

2. What gives you the strength and the will to respond in obedience?

3. What is the role of prayer in answering God's call?

4. What changes will you make in your prayer life as a result of this study?

5. How has this journey of personal revival made a difference in your life?

Wrapping Up

What assignment has God given you? Would you ask Him? I know He has one in mind for you because He told us clearly, through the words of the apostle Paul, that "we are God's workmanship, created in Christ Jesus to do good works, which God prepared in advance for us to do."

Don't dodge your assignment because it seems to lack any chance for success. Don't miss your assignment because it seems such an insignificant, small thing.... The size and scope of the assignment are up to Him, and the effectiveness and lasting impact of your service are also His responsibility. You and I are simply to be faithfully available ... and obedient.

Expecting to See Jesus, p. 190

God has called each and every one of us into action. We must respond in obedient faith so that He will continue the work of revival He has already begun in our lives. God wants us not only to hear His Word, but to live by it. He will walk with us, but we must move our feet!

As you complete this revival journey, take time to surrender to Him for service. What is the still, small voice of the Father asking you to do for Him? What burden, idea, or vision has He placed on your heart as an opportunity for service?

The time has come to step out. Move your feet! As you do, keep the eyes of your heart open! Expect to see Jesus!

Expecting to See Jesus

A Wake-Up Call for God's People

Anne Graham Lotz

Expecting to See Jesus—the expanded edition of *I Saw the LORD*—is the result of Anne Graham Lotz's life lived in the hope of Jesus' return. As you journey with her through the pages of the Bible, you'll come to realize why she lives her life expecting to see Jesus at any minute.

And, she wants to make sure you and all other Christians are ready for that moment when your faith becomes sight.

Anne knows from personal experience that it's in the busyness of our days, as we're drifting in comfortable complacency, that we most need a wake-up call—a jolt that pushes us to seek out a revival of our passion for Jesus that began as a blazing fire but somehow has died down to an ineffective glow.

In *Expecting to See Jesus*, Anne points out the biblical signs she sees in the world all around us and shows how you can experience an authentic, deeper, richer relationship with God in a life-changing, fire-blazing revival.